# SEXUALLY TRANSMITTED DISEASES

Jo Whelan

HODDER
*Wayland*

an imprint of Hodder Children's Books

© 2001 White-Thomson Publishing Ltd

White-Thomson Publishing Ltd,
2-3 St Andrew's Place, Lewes,
East Sussex BN7 1UP

Published in Great Britain in 2001 by Hodder
Wayland, an imprint of Hodder Children's
Books
This paperback edition published in 2002

This book was produced for White-Thomson
Publishing Ltd by Ruth Nason.

Design: Carole Binding
Picture research: Glass Onion Pictures

The right of Jo Whelan to be identified as the
author of this work has been asserted by her in
accordance with the Copyright, Designs and
Patents Act 1988.

British Library Cataloguing in Publication Data
Whelan, Jo
    Sexually Transmitted Diseases. - (Health
    Issues)
    1. Sexually Transmitted Diseases - Juvenile
    literature
    I. Title
    616.9'51

ISBN 0 7502 3544 6

Printed in Hong Kong by Wing King Tong Co. Ltd.

Hodder Children's Books
A division of Hodder Headline Limited
338 Euston Road, London NW1 3BH

## Acknowledgements

The author and publishers thank the following for their permission to reproduce photographs and
illustrations: Associated Press: page 9; Camera Press: pages 6, 26, 49; Corbis Images: pages 5t
(Lester V. Bergman), 7 (David Turnley), 13 (Jennie Woodcock; Reflections Photolibrary), 14 (Left Lane
Productions), 20 (Wartenberg/Picture Press), 32, 52 (Bettmann), 53; Howard Davies: page 12; Angela
Hampton Family Life Picture Library: cover, pages 1, 15, 27, 31, 38; Robert Harding Picture Library:
page 44; Impact Photos: pages 4b (John Cole), 11 (Rachel Morton); National Medical Slide Bank:
pages 37, 40; Photofusion: page 8 (Christa Stadtler); Popperfoto: pages 23, 46, 50; Chris Schwarz:
page 10; Science Photo Library: pages 4t (NIBSC), 5b (Eye of Science), 16 (Gary Parker), 19 (Saturn
Stills), 28 (Dr R. Dourmashkin), 30 (John Bavosi), 33 (NRI), 34 (Mauro Fermariello), 35 (Tek Image),
36 (Alfred Pasteka), 39 (Em Unit, VLA), 43 (D. Phillips), 45 (NIBSC), 55 (BSIP/Custom Medical Stock
Photo),m 57 (Eye of Science); Topham/Novosti: page 18; Topham Picturepoint: pages 25, 54;
Wayland Picture Library (Michael Courtney): pages 21, 22.

# Contents

**Introduction**
A hidden epidemic                                          4

**1  Are you at risk?**
Who gets STDs and how they are spread                      8

**2  Preventing STDs**
Choices and responsibilities                              14

**3  Symptoms and treatment**
When to seek help                                         20

**4  Common STDs**
Causes, symptoms and treatment                            28

**5  Other STDs**
Causes, symptoms and treatment                            44

**Glossary**                                              60

**Resources**                                             62

**Index**                                                 63

# Introduction
# A hidden epidemic

Sexually transmitted diseases, or STDs, are infections that are spread from person to person by sexual contact. An old name for them was venereal diseases (VD), 'venereal' being from the Latin word for sexual love. Nowadays they are often called sexually transmitted infections, or STIs.

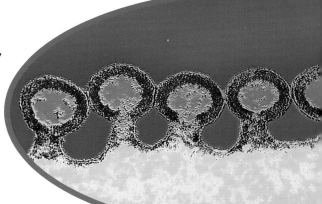

STDs have probably been around almost as long as sex itself. A disease like gonorrhoea was recorded over 2,000 years ago, and there was a major epidemic of syphilis in the fifteenth to early twentieth centuries. In contrast, HIV (the virus that causes AIDS) only came onto the scene in the 1970s but is now a major killer in many parts of the world.

**Viruses**
*This is a false-colour electron micrograph of HIV viruses budding from the surface of a white blood cell.*

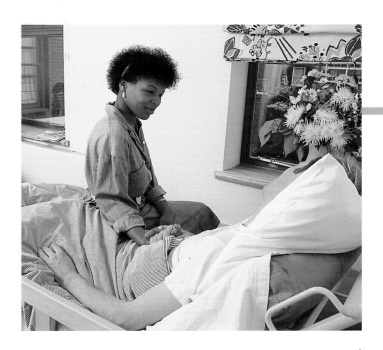

**AIDS**
*AIDS stands for Acquired Immuno-deficiency Syndrome. It is the most devastating of all sexually transmitted diseases.*

## What causes STDs?

Some STDs are caused by bacteria, some by viruses and some by tiny parasites ranging from microscopic organisms to lice. What these all have in common is a liking for the genital (sexual) areas of the human body. They are fragile organisms which don't survive for long away from the body or body fluids. Some of them live on the external skin and others in the tissues of the vagina and penis and in body fluids like semen, vaginal fluids and blood. When an infected person has sexual intercourse or close sexual contact, the STD 'bugs' can move across and infect his or her partner.

### Bacteria

*This electron micrograph shows syphilis bacteria.*

## Bacteria, viruses and parasites

*Bacteria consist of a single cell, complete with everything it needs to live and reproduce. They can be killed by antibiotic drugs, although some bacteria have adapted to become drug-resistant.*

*Viruses are made of nothing but some strands of genetic material (DNA or RNA), a protein coat and sometimes an outer 'envelope'. They cannot reproduce without the help of cells from their host (the plant or animal they have infected). It is very difficult to kill them without damaging the host cell as well, so there are few anti-viral drugs available.*

*Parasites are animals which rely on their host for food, for example by sucking its blood.*

### Parasites

*These parasites are pubic lice (an adult and a juvenile) hanging from human pubic hair. They feed by sucking blood, and cause severe itching.*

## What do STDs do?

The effects of STDs range from unnoticeable through to mild symptoms through to serious illness and even death. For many people the infection is 'silent'; they have no noticeable symptoms but can still be infectious to others. Sometimes, a silent infection stays hidden in the body and slowly damages it, producing health problems months or years after it was caught.

When STDs do produce symptoms, these usually show up in the genital area as abnormal discharge, pain, itching, sores or warts. HIV, hepatitis B and syphilis cause illnesses that affect the whole body.

## How common are STDs?

STDs are a very common problem. About 1 person in 4 will pick one up by the time they are 25. Young people run the highest risk: two-thirds of all sexually transmitted diseases happen in people aged under 25, and a quarter in the 15-19 age group. In the USA alone, 4 million teenagers get an STD every year.

### AIDS vigil

*These people are marking World AIDS Day. Because it is so terrifying, most of us know about AIDS. But there is less awareness about other STDs.*

## About this book

STDs have been called a 'hidden epidemic'. Surveys show that many people know very little about them, and most underestimate how common they are. This is partly because, despite the sexual imagery we see everywhere, society is still embarrassed about discussing the realities of sex. This book aims to give you clear information about the different STDs and how they are spread, the risk of infection and what you can do to protect yourself if you choose to have sex.

Chapter 1 looks at how STDs are spread and who is most at risk, and chapter 2 discusses how they can be prevented. Chapter 3 covers symptoms and treatment. Chapters 4 and 5 describe each STD in turn, giving details of how common they are, how they are spread, their symptoms and how they are treated. Sources of help and information are listed on page 62, and the glossary on page 60 explains the less familiar words used.

## Could STDs affect me?

*If you are sexually active, you are at risk from STDs. They affect people of all ages, races and backgrounds. The more sexual partners you have, the greater your chance of getting one, especially if you don't use condoms. But STDs don't just affect people who 'sleep around'; it only takes sex with one infected person to pick up the disease yourself. Like unplanned pregnancy, the risk of STDs is something that everyone should think about before having sex.*

# 1 Are you at risk?
## Who gets STDs and how they are spread

Anyone who is sexually active can get an STD, unless neither they nor their partner has ever had sex with anyone else. STDs don't just affect prostitutes, drug users or people who 'sleep around' – though these groups are at high risk. About 1 person in 3 will pick up a sexually transmitted disease at some time in their life, though many will be unaware of it because they will not notice any symptoms.

**Myth** | **Fact**

*If someone had an STD, I would be able to tell.* | *Many people with STDs have no visible symptoms. Often they do not even realize that they are infected.*

**Young people**
*Under-25s are the age group most at risk of STDs.*

Although anyone can get an STD, some types of behaviour put you at higher risk:

⬤ Having sex with lots of different people. The more partners you have, the greater your chance of going with someone who has an STD – which then gets passed on to you.

⬤ Having sex with someone who has had lots of partners. When you have sex with someone, it is as though you are also having sex with everyone else that person has ever been with! If any of their earlier partners had an STD, then your partner is likely to have caught it too, and you are the next in line.

⬤ Having sex without using a condom. Condoms (rubbers) give good protection against many (but not all) STDs. See chapter 2 for details.

⬤ Buying or selling sex: people who sell sex (e.g. prostitutes or rent boys) are at high risk because they have many different partners. They also pass STDs to their clients.

⬤ Injecting drugs, or having sex with people who do. Drug users who share needles are at high risk of HIV and hepatitis, which are passed on through blood on the needles. These diseases can be passed on to their sexual partners.

**Safer sex**

*As part of a campaign promoting safer sex, packets of condoms were given to motor-cyclists in Bangkok, Thailand, on St Valentine's Day, 2000.*

## Teens at risk

Which age groups have the highest risk of getting an STD? The answer may surprise you – it is teenagers aged 15-19 and young adults up to 24. The statistics are worrying:

- Teenagers account for around a quarter of all new STD infections.
- 25 per cent of sexually active teens pick up an STD each year.
- One person in four will get an STD by the time they are 25.
- Women aged 15-19 have the highest rate of gonorrhoea of any group in the USA; in men, 15-19 is the age group with the second highest rate.
- Chlamydia has been found in 5-20 per cent of sexually active teenage girls and around 10 per cent of sexually active teenage boys.
- Clinics are treating STDs in children as young as 11.

### Demonstration

*For teenagers, doctors and clinics recommend the 'double Dutch' method of contraception (using both the contraceptive pill and condoms). Here, a condom is being demonstrated.*

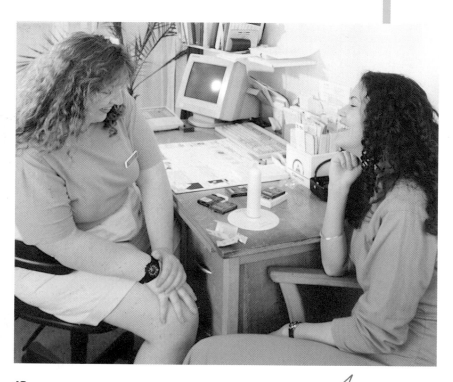

Doctors think there are several reasons why STDs are so common in teens and young adults. These groups are less likely to be in stable, long-term relationships and more likely to have a number of different sexual partners. Teenagers are probably less likely than older people to use a condom when having sex with a new partner. And teenagers are less likely to get testing and treatment for STDs because they are nervous about going to clinics, worried that their parents will find out or, in some countries, worried about the cost. We will discuss treatment in chapter 3.

*'I knew I ought to get some condoms, but it took me ages to pluck up courage to go in to the chemist's to buy them. I felt so self-conscious!'*
*(Mark, 16)*

The figures show that STDs are not 'someone else's problem'. For teenagers who choose to have sex, they are an issue that cannot be ignored. The good news is that most STDs can be prevented, as we will see in chapter 2.

## Risks for women

*Both sexes are at risk from STDs, but the infections have some particular effects for women:*

- 🌐 *Some STDs, if untreated, can spread further into a woman's reproductive system, causing long-term pain and affecting her ability to have children (see page 30).*
- 🌐 *Some types of human papilloma virus can cause cervical cancer.*
- 🌐 *Many STDs can be passed from a pregnant woman to her baby, sometimes causing serious illness or disability. Some infections also increase the risk of miscarriage and premature birth.*

### Routine screening
*In the UK, pregnant women are routinely screened on their first blood test for syphilis, hepatitis B and HIV. The tests are never done without the person's permission.*

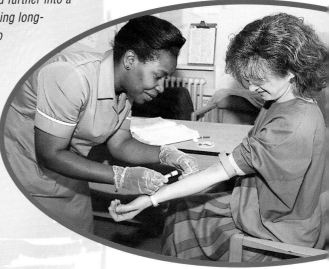

## How are STDs spread?

Different infections are spread in different ways, depending on the bacteria, virus or parasite that causes them. Details for each disease are given in chapters 4 and 5. Most STD bacteria and viruses live in the tissues and fluids of the vagina and penis, and sometimes the anus as well. Some live in the semen (sperm fluid), and HIV and hepatitis B also live in the blood. Others (herpes and human papilloma virus) live on or just below the skin. The skin is also home to parasites like pubic lice and scabies. Because STD bugs have a range of lifestyles, any type of sexual contact can potentially spread infection.

Having one STD makes it easier to pick up another, because infected tissue is more vulnerable to germs. So people often have more than one infection. For example, gonorrhoea and chlamydia often go together.

The most common way for STDs to spread is through sharing body fluids during vaginal sex (the penis entering

**Men**
*Men who have sex with men run a higher than average risk of getting STDs, especially HIV.*

the vagina) or anal sex (the penis entering the anus, either of a woman or of another man). The man does not have to 'come' (release sperm) for infection to be passed on. Just rubbing the penis on the outer vagina or anus, without penetration, could be enough for a disease to spread. Some STDs can also spread by oral sex (using the mouth to stimulate the partner's genitals).

The other main method of spread is skin-to-skin contact between partners' genital areas, whether during full intercourse or other types of sex play. This can spread herpes, genital warts, syphilis, scabies and molluscum contagiosum. Pubic lice move from the pubic hair of one person to another. Scabies, molluscum contagiosum and pubic lice can occasionally be passed on by sharing bedding, clothes or towels with an infected person.

## Myth | Fact

*You can catch STDs from toilet seats.* | *STD bugs need a warm, moist place to live – like a body. They can't survive on their own for long. You can't catch them from toilets or other objects (except the examples given above), swimming pools, kissing, clothed hugging or mosquito bites.*

### Being prepared
*Knowing the facts about STDs is important when making choices about sexual behaviour.*

# 2 Preventing STDs
## Choices and responsibilities

Everyone who is sexually active should be aware of the risk from sexually transmitted diseases. However, there is no need to let fear of STDs spoil things if and when you decide to have a sexual relationship. In this chapter, we will look at ways of avoiding them.

### Saying 'no' to sex

Teenagers often feel under a lot of pressure to have sex. Talk among friends, images on TV and stories in magazines can make it seem as though everyone is doing it – though many teenagers, especially those still of school age, are not. Deciding when to have sex is very personal, and it's a decision that should be made carefully, never as a result of pressure from other people, or under the influence of alcohol or drugs.

**!**

**Fact**
*The only 100% effective way to avoid catching an STD is not to have sex!*

**All talk**
*Groups of girls or boys sometimes talk as if they are much more 'experienced' than they really are.*

Choosing not to have sex for a while is called abstinence. Most people go through periods of abstinence, even as adults. There are many reasons why it can be the right choice:

- to avoid risk of unplanned pregnancy or sexually transmitted disease
- because you are not feeling emotionally or physically ready
- because you are not with the right person
- to stay true to religious or other personal beliefs.

There are lots of ways of enjoying physical contact without having full sex. Limiting your relationship to hugging, kissing and touching carries a lower risk of getting an STD, though it does not remove the risk entirely.

*'I've got my whole life ahead of me to experiment with sex. What's the hurry to start now?'*
*(Jim, 14)*

### Julie

*Julie is 15 and has had a couple of boyfriends. These relationships involved quite a lot of kissing and touching, but Julie has stopped short of having sex – even though one of her boyfriends put her under a lot of pressure to 'go all the way'. Looking back, she is glad she didn't. 'When I have sex for the first time I want it to be special,' she says. 'I want to feel completely ready for it and I want it to be with someone I love. I know people who've lost their virginity when they were drunk, with some guy they didn't even like that much. Afterwards they just thought, "oh, so that's it then". It wasn't really a big deal, and I think that's sad.' She doesn't mind being a virgin. 'I'm not going to have sex just to prove that I'm cool. I want a better reason than that.'*

## Faithful relationships

Couples where neither partner has ever had sex with anyone else have no risk of STDs. Similarly, when two people decide to have sex only with each other, they are safe unless one of them is already infected from a previous relationship. If either partner is worried about this, it's a good idea to get tested before you stop using condoms.

## Casual sex

Some people get into the habit of having sex with lots of different partners, perhaps people they have only just met. This lifestyle puts you at high risk of picking up an STD, especially if you don't always use condoms. It can also leave you feeling empty inside, because the love and friendship that are part of the most fulfilling sex are missing.

### Fact

*The more sexual partners you have, the greater your risk of getting an STD.*

## Safer sex

If you decide to have sex, it is important to protect yourself from STDs – and, of course, from unplanned pregnancy. Pregnancy can be prevented by various methods, including contraceptive pills, implants or injections, caps or

### Alison and Craig

*Alison and Craig met at college a year ago. Over the months they both began to realize that the relationship was special, and now they've decided to move in together. Ever since catching chlamydia as a teenager, Alison has been strict about using condoms. However, Craig has had 'quite a few girlfriends' in the past, including some one-night stands, and often didn't bother with a condom because the girls were on the Pill. Now Alison wants them both to get a sexual health checkup before they stop using condoms and she goes onto the Pill. Craig has agreed. 'I suppose part of me did feel a bit hurt at first, as though she didn't trust me. But I can see it from her point of view, and I respect that. I've taken what you might call some stupid risks, and I don't want Alison to end up paying the price. If you love someone you want to protect them, so I don't mind taking the tests.'*

diaphragms, and condoms. But *only condoms* give protection against STDs. This is because they form a barrier between the skin of the two partners and prevent their sexual fluids from entering each other's bodies. Even if you are using another birth control method, you should use a condom as well – unless you are in a faithful, long-term relationship where both partners are free from STDs.

**Putting on a condom**

# How to use a condom

*Condoms are only effective if used properly. Here's how to do it:*

- Put the condom on the erect (hard) penis before any contact with the partner's genitals.

- Place the rolled-up condom on the tip of the penis and pinch the end of the condom between your thumb and finger so that it does not fill with air. This leaves room for the sperm to flow into.

- Roll the condom down the penis right to the base, pulling the foreskin (hood) back gently to expose the penis tip.

- If the condom is not lubricated, moisten it with a water-based lubricant (you can buy these at the pharmacy). Don't use oil-based lubricants like Vaseline, baby oil or hand cream as these can weaken the condom.

- When withdrawing the penis after sex, hold the base of the condom to stop it falling off. Do this before the penis goes soft.

- Only use approved condom brands. Novelty condoms may not be effective. Condoms made from animal skin don't protect against STDs.

- Use an extra-strong brand of condom for anal sex.

- Don't use out-of-date condoms – check the expiry date on the packet.

- Use a new condom each time.

## How effective are condoms?

Studies have shown that latex (rubber) and polyurethane condoms give very effective protection against STDs that are spread through sexual fluids or blood. In couples where one partner has HIV, condoms are 98-100 per cent effective at stopping the other partner from catching it. To get this level of protection, it is essential to use the condom correctly and to use it from start to finish every time you have vaginal, anal or oral sex.

Condoms are less effective against diseases spread by skin-to-skin contact, for example herpes and genital warts. This is because the infectious skin can be outside the area covered by the condom. However, the condom does give some protection.

**Production line**
*Manufacturers produce a wide range of condoms, including 'novelty' ones, to make them appealing to use. Always check the packet for the mark of official quality approval.*

## Talking about safer sex

Sex can have serious consequences: you could get pregnant, become a father or catch an STD, perhaps even a disease that stays with you for life. It's your responsibility to look after yourself and make sure these things don't happen. Many people find it embarrassing to talk to a new partner about safer sex, but it's better to be a little embarrassed than to end up pregnant or get an STD!

If you are planning to have sex, or think you might, it's up to you to bring the condoms – whether you are male or female. Don't just assume that your partner will have some. Women often feel awkward about carrying condoms, in case people think they are out looking for sex. This old-fashioned idea is sexist and hypocritical. Being prepared doesn't make you 'cheap'; instead, it shows that you take responsibility for your own sexual health.

It helps to be clear in advance about your sexual limits, and to stick to them. Any partner who respects you will understand that you want to protect yourself; and after all, using a condom will protect them too. Remind them that anyone can get an STD and not know about it – insisting on a condom doesn't mean that you don't trust them or think they sleep around.

*'I don't have sex without condoms. That's the deal.'*
*(Lynne, 17)*

## Sexual health checkups

If you think you have put yourself at risk of an STD, it is a good idea to have a sexual health checkup, even if you don't have any symptoms. Ask your doctor or local STD clinic – details of how to find these are given on page 25. You can be tested for the common diseases, and treated if necessary. This will help prevent long-term damage to your health, and stop you passing any diseases on. In particular, many doctors recommend that sexually active teenage girls should be tested for chlamydia every 6-12 months. If you have any symptoms that might be an STD, see your doctor or clinic straight away.

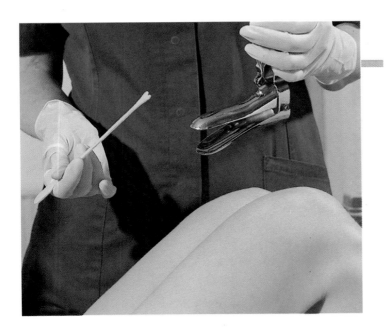

## Smear test

*All sexually active women should have regular cervical smear tests. The doctor or nurse inserts the speculum (with its 'bill' closed) gently into the vagina, then widens the bill to open the vagina in order to examine the cervix and scrape some cells from it for testing.*

# 3 Symptoms and treatment
## When to seek help

How do you know if you have a sexually transmitted disease? The answer is that, often, you don't. Many people with STDs have no symptoms, at least at the beginning. When symptoms do occur they can be very mild, so it's easier to ignore them than do something about it. After a few weeks the problem may clear up and is quickly forgotten. But sometimes the bacteria or virus is still there, ready to infect sexual partners and perhaps doing silent damage that will lead to illness later.

When STDs do give symptoms they can range from annoying, to very unpleasant, to serious or even (in the long term) fatal.

**Myth**

*I'm sexually active but I feel fine. I've got nothing to worry about.*

**Fact**

*Many STDs cause no symptoms, at least at the beginning. But people with no symptoms can still infect others, and may be at risk of long-term damage to their health.*

## Symptoms in men

The following can all be symptoms of an STD in men. These symptoms can also have other causes that are nothing to do with STDs. The diagram shows the parts of the body.

- Discharge (abnormal fluid) from the penis
- Itching, soreness or redness at the penis tip
- Pain when having sex
- Pain or burning sensation when peeing
- Needing to pee unusually often
- Sores, warts, itching or rash on the genitals, upper thighs, buttocks or anus
- Discharge or pain from the anus
- Pain or swelling in the scrotum
- Sores or white patches in the mouth or throat
- Flu-like symptoms or swollen glands

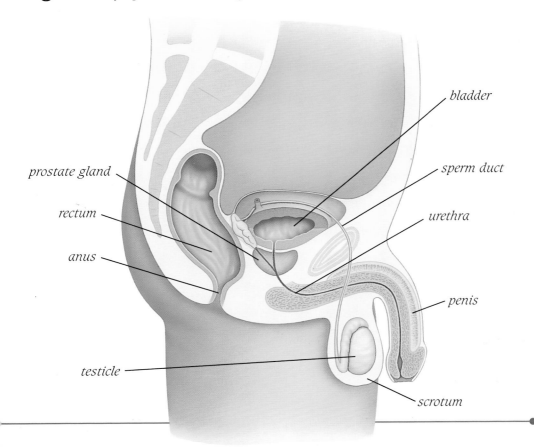

prostate gland

rectum

anus

testicle

bladder

sperm duct

urethra

penis

scrotum

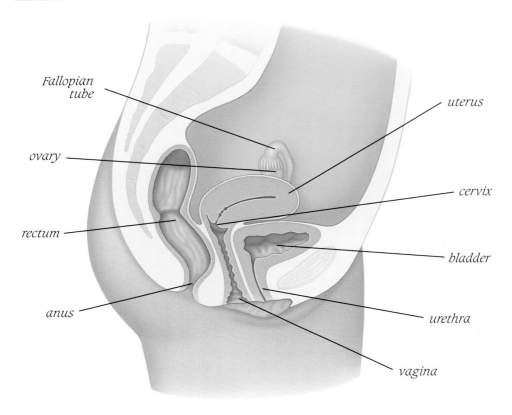

*Fallopian tube*

*ovary*

*rectum*

*anus*

*uterus*

*cervix*

*bladder*

*urethra*

*vagina*

## Symptoms in women

The following can all be symptoms of an STD in women. They can also have other causes. The parts of the body are shown in the diagram.

- ⊛ Unusual discharge (fluid) from the vagina
- ⊛ Pain when having sex
- ⊛ Discharge from the urethra (urinary tract)
- ⊛ Pain or burning sensation when peeing
- ⊛ Needing to pee unusually often
- ⊛ Pain or tenderness in the abdomen (belly)
- ⊛ Sores, warts, itching or rash in the vagina, vulva, upper thighs, buttocks or anus
- ⊛ Discharge or pain from the anus
- ⊛ Sores or white patches in the mouth or throat
- ⊛ Flu-like symptoms or swollen glands

Most of the symptoms listed can have lots of different causes, and not everyone with a particular disease experiences the same effects. Because of this, only a doctor can tell you whether you have an STD, and which one it is.

## Feelings about STDs

Getting an STD can be unpleasant emotionally as well as physically. People may feel ashamed or dirty, or angry at their partner for infecting them. They may be put off sex or find it difficult to trust new partners. If it is a disease that cannot be cured, they must come to terms with having the infection for the rest of their life – and, in the case of HIV, with the probability of serious illness in the future.

*'I used to be carefree about sex, but now when I meet someone I think "what's she got?" Last time I slept with someone I almost didn't get an erection because I couldn't stop thinking about it.'*
*(Jason, 18)*

**Feelings**
*The discovery of an STD can challenge a couple's relationship.*

## Treating STDs

It's important to see a doctor if you are sexually active and have any of the symptoms listed, or any other symptoms that worry you. The sooner you get treatment, the less likely you are to suffer long-term effects or infect other people. And knowing for certain what infection you do or don't have is usually better than worrying about it.

Sometimes the doctor will be able to diagnose the problem just by examining you and asking questions about your symptoms. In other cases they will need to do a blood or urine test or send a sample away to a laboratory. It's natural to find these things embarrassing, but remember that the doctor has seen and heard it all many times before, and won't be embarrassed or shocked.

### Amy

*A week after having sex with Stewart for the first time, Amy started to get a painful burning sensation when she peed. Then she noticed a heavier than usual discharge from her vagina, and the whole area became tender and sore. She knew something was wrong and thought it might be an STD: 'I worried myself sick about what I might have caught.'*

*Ignoring the problem didn't make it go away, so Amy plucked up courage to see her doctor. The doctor suggested that, if an STD was a possibility, it would really be better to go to a GUM clinic. 'She explained what that was and why it was better, then made contact with them for me and arranged for me to go.'*

*At the clinic the doctor took a swab and the laboratory looked at the sample. It showed that Amy had gonorrhoea. The treatment would be a single antibiotic tablet. 'It was such a relief when I knew what it was. The antibiotic cleared it up in a couple of days, and the doctor said we'd caught it in time to stop the infection spreading further inside me. The clinic sent Stewart a note saying he should be tested; I don't know if he went.'*

Prevention is better than cure. Instead of treating STDs, it is better not to get them in the first place. See chapter 2 for ways to protect yourself.

## Where can I go for help?

Your family doctor (GP) will be used to helping people with STDs. You may be referred to a specialist clinic for tests. Since the organisms that cause STDs do not survive for long outside the body, it is better for the clinic to take swabs and analyse them, rather than the swab being taken at the doctor's surgery and sent away. The doctor will not tell your parents without your permission, even if you are under 16.

You can also go to an NHS sexual health clinic – these are also known as STD clinics and genito-urinary medicine or GUM clinics. You can find the number of your nearest clinic in the telephone book under STD or 'genito-urinary', or by phoning the switchboard of your local hospital. These clinics do free testing and treatment and are completely confidential. They also offer sexual health checks to anyone who wants one.

### Helplines

See page 62 for details of helplines and Web sites that give information and advice on STDs.

*'I was really, really nervous about going to the clinic. I thought it would be like getting told off by a teacher or something. But they treated me like an adult and didn't give lectures, although they did give me information about safer sex.'*
*(Steve, 15)*

## Can STDs be cured?

Many can, but some can't. Treatments for individual diseases are discussed in chapters 4 and 5. In general, infections caused by bacteria can be cured with antibiotics. This kills the bacteria completely and leaves the person free of infection. However, antibiotics can't repair any damage the bacteria have already done – for example, they can't get rid of scarring caused by pelvic inflammatory disease (see page 30). Many STDs can be caught more than once, and treatment does not stop you being infected again. Different bacteria respond to different antibiotics, so don't rely on antibiotics prescribed for a sore throat to cure an STD as well. It's important to take the full course – don't stop before the end just because the symptoms seem better, as some bacteria could be left alive.

Infections caused by parasites are also fully curable. Your doctor will know which drugs work against which infections.

Viruses are more difficult to tackle. Some viral infections, like colds and flu, are short-lasting and our bodies deal with them on their own. Others – including HIV, herpes,

### Drugs

*Nowadays, many STDs can be cured or partially controlled with drugs. Someone with HIV might have to take all these pills every day for life.*

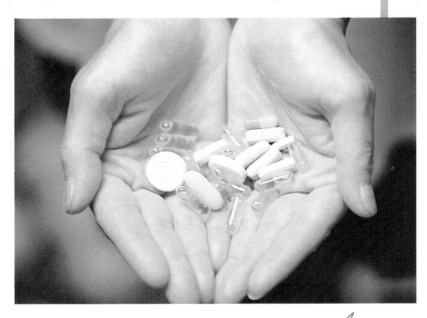

some cases of hepatitis B and probably human papilloma virus – stay around in the body. There are currently no drugs which can kill and remove them, so the infection lasts for life. Drugs can sometimes stop the virus reproducing or make its symptoms less severe. Sometimes the virus stays inactive and harmless without the need for any treatment.

## What about sexual partners?

Although STDs are very personal, they are also a shared problem. Someone with an STD has either picked it up from their sexual partner or is likely to pass it on to them. Either way, recent partners need to be tested and treated for the following reasons:

- for their own health
- to stop them passing the infection to others
- to stop the current partner from being reinfected after treatment.

Telling partners is not easy: you may feel guilty towards them, or you may feel angry that they have infected you. Try to overcome these feelings. Remember that most infections are passed on without the infectious person being aware of it. An STD does not necessarily mean that someone has been unfaithful; it could have been picked up months or years ago.

Your doctor or clinic will talk over the best way to notify your partner or partners. If you want, the clinic can send contact slips telling people that they may have been exposed to an STD and advising them to come for a test. Your name is not given. The clinic will not do anything without your consent.

## Thinking it through
*There's a lot to think through if you or your partner is diagnosed with an STD.*

# 4 Common STDs
## Causes, symptoms and treatment

This chapter deals with the STDs that are most common today in the developed world.

## Chlamydia

Chlamydia is caused by bacteria called *Chlamydia trachomatis*. It is spread during sexual intercourse when the penis enters the vagina, anus or mouth. A woman having unprotected sex with an infected man stands about a 40 per cent chance of catching chlamydia each time they have intercourse. (Unprotected means without using a

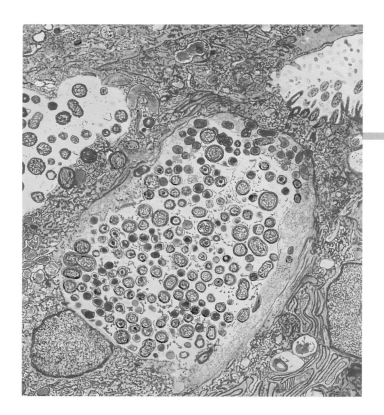

**Chlamydia**
*This false-colour electron micrograph shows a cross-section of cells in a woman's Fallopian tube infected with chlamydia bacteria. These bacteria (the green/brown circles) live only inside cells (yellow).*

condom.) If the woman is infected, the man's chance of infection each time is about 20 per cent. Chlamydia is one of the most common STDs: 3-4 million new cases occur each year in the USA, and in the UK it is thought to affect about 1 in 20 sexually active people under the age of 25.

*'I've never heard of chlamydia. I don't think most teenagers are aware of it.' (Nikki, 17)*

Chlamydia is a big problem in teenagers and young adults. The highest rates of infection occur in women aged 15-19. Because most people don't realize they are infected, the disease carries on spreading. For men it is usually fairly harmless, but in women chlamydia can cause serious long-term problems unless treated early.

### Symptoms and effects

Chlamydia produces no symptoms in about 75 per cent of infected women and 50 per cent of men. When it does, they develop 1-3 weeks after infection and can be quite mild. They sometimes clear up on their own within four weeks. Women may get a yellowish vaginal discharge, pain when peeing or having sex, bleeding from the vagina or pain in the lower abdomen. Men experience a discharge from the penis, and/or pain when peeing. Chlamydia infection in men is sometimes called non-specific urethritis, or NSU (see page 35). In either sex, the anus or throat can be painful and have a yellow discharge if these areas have been infected.

## Recurrent infection

*According to the US Centers for Disease Control and Prevention, recurrent chlamydia infections are a very serious problem, especially in teenagers. Recurrent means that someone catches chlamydia several times, perhaps from different sexual partners or perhaps from the same one. Doctors know that each time the infection comes back its effects are more severe, with a greater likelihood of complications like those described on page 30.*

The serious effects of chlamydia occur when it spreads further into the reproductive system. This can happen even if the person is free from symptoms to begin with, and carries on after the initial symptoms clear up. In women it can cause pelvic inflammatory disease (PID), and this can lead to infertility.

## Pelvic inflammatory disease

In women, chlamydia and gonorrhoea infections can travel up from the cervix and affect the uterus, Fallopian tubes and ovaries. This is called pelvic inflammatory disease (PID), and develops in around one third of women who catch chlamydia. (PID also has other causes that are not sexually transmitted.) PID can cause chronic pain in the abdomen, pain when having sex and bleeding between periods.

Sometimes the Fallopian tubes become blocked by scars from the infection, and therefore eggs cannot travel from the ovaries to the uterus. This makes the woman unable to conceive children. About 20 per cent of women with PID become infertile. Another risk is that a fertilized egg will become trapped in the scarred Fallopian tube and begin to develop there, instead of in the uterus. This is called an ectopic pregnancy, and is very dangerous. If it is not detected and removed, the developing embryo eventually bursts the tube, causing great pain and potentially fatal internal bleeding.

### Ectopic pregnancy
*One risk of PID is that the woman will have an ectopic pregnancy, where the embryo develops in the Fallopian tube rather than in the uterus.*

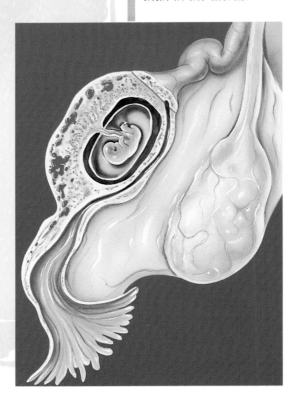

## Michelle

*Michelle and Mark have been married for two years, and for the last 18 months they have been trying unsuccessfully for a baby. Tests at the infertility clinic have shown that Michelle has pelvic inflammatory disease (PID), which has blocked her Fallopian tubes. This means that eggs released from her ovaries can't reach her uterus. The doctor thinks the PID was probably caused by chlamydia. 'It was a total shock,' says Michelle, 'I had no idea that anything was wrong. For the last three years I've only slept with Mark, but I suppose I wasn't very careful when I was younger. I was on the Pill, but I didn't really think about protecting myself from STDs. Of course it could have been Mark who gave it to me, we just don't know. I'm having an operation to try and unblock my tubes; if that doesn't work, our only hope of having a baby is through IVF – you know, a test-tube baby.'*

Men have a much lower risk than women of long-term effects from chlamydia, but in 1-2 per cent of cases it causes epididymitis, a painful inflammation and swelling in the scrotum. In rare cases this can cause infertility if not treated. Despite the low risk of serious effects, it is still important for men with chlamydia to get treatment, to stop them infecting their female partners.

A pregnant woman who has chlamydia can pass the infection to her baby as it is born. Affected babies may suffer infections of the eye (conjunctivitis) or lungs (pneumonia).

### Testing and treatment

Chlamydia is diagnosed either by testing the urine or by analysing a sample taken from the cervix or penis. The doctor will wipe the area with a swab, which is sent to a laboratory to be analysed. Because of the health risks, many doctors recommend that sexually active young women should be tested for chlamydia every 6-12 months. However, there is much debate about this recommendation, and whether both men and women should be routinely tested.

Chlamydia is easily treated with antibiotics. But although these get rid of the infection, they cannot undo any damage that may already have been caused by PID. So it is important to seek treatment as quickly as possible if you notice symptoms, and to consider regular testing. Chlamydia can be caught more than once; using condoms will prevent reinfection.

## Gonorrhoea

Gonorrhoea is caused by bacteria called *Neisseria gonorrhoeae*. It is the oldest known STD; its common nickname, the 'clap', originated in the 14th century. From the mid-1970s onwards, at a time when many other STDs were on the increase, the number of cases of gonorrhoea fell. The only group where infection rates rose was 15-19 year-olds, probably because they became more sexually active.

Gonorrhoea is spread by vaginal, oral or anal sex and by genital contact. Using a condom gives good protection but does not cut out the risk completely. A woman having unprotected sex with an infected man has an 80-90 per cent chance of catching it each time they have

**Two 'girls'**
*This American wartime poster warned soldiers against sex with prostitutes. The 'two girls' who 'want to meet' the soldier are Gonorrhoea and Syphilis.*

"Two girls I know want to meet you in the worst way."

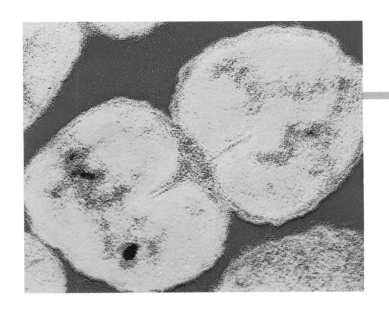

### Gonorrhoea

*Gonorrhoea bacteria are of the round type known as cocci.*

intercourse. For a man, the risk of catching gonorrhoea from an infected woman is 20-25 per cent each time.

## Symptoms and effects

In about 50 per cent of women and a third of men, gonorrhoea produces no immediate symptoms at all. This means a person can be infected – and infectious to others – without knowing about it. Even symptom-free infections can have serious effects later on.

When symptoms occur they develop 2-10 days after sex with the infected person. The most common symptom in men is a burning sensation when peeing, which can range from mild to extremely painful. They may want to pee more often than usual. There is usually a yellowish discharge from the penis, and the opening can be red and sore. In women the first symptoms are usually mild, with pain or burning when peeing and sometimes a yellowish discharge from the vagina. The rectum can be affected in either sex, either from anal intercourse or, in women, if the bacteria spread from the vagina. The anal area becomes red, sore or itchy, and there is often a discharge. Bowel movements may be painful.

Gonorrhoea bacteria can also cause eye infections. This might happen if an infected person rubbed their eyes after touching their genitals. It is also possible for the babies of women with gonorrhoea to be infected during birth. These eye infections can cause blindness if not treated.

In some women, the bacteria travel further into the reproductive system and affect the Fallopian tubes, ovaries and uterus. This is called pelvic inflammatory disease (PID), which is described on page 30. PID can cause chronic pain and infertility.

### Testing and treatment

Many STD clinics can identify gonorrhoea using a urine test which looks for fragments of the bacteria's genetic material (DNA). Another test involves smearing some of the discharge from the penis or vagina onto a microscope slide and treating it with a chemical stain which shows up the bacteria. This is called a Gram test, and usually produces an instant result. It is more effective in men than in women. Sometimes a discharge sample is placed onto a special jelly to see if the gonorrhoea bacteria will grow there. This is known as a culture test, and results take a couple of days. The doctor will often test for chlamydia at the same time, because the two infections are often spread together.

Gonorrhoea can be successfully treated with antibiotics. It is important to use the right drug, because the disease has become resistant to some treatments.

**Checking slides**
*Microscope slides of stained tissue samples (in this case from smear tests) are checked in the laboratory.*

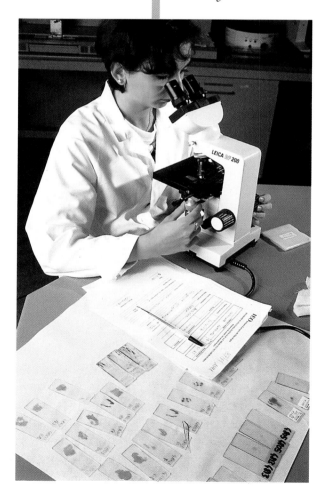

## Non-specific urethritis (NSU)

NSU is the name sometimes given to inflammation of the urethra (urine pipe) in men when it is caused by bacterial infections other than gonorrhoea. The name non-gonococcal urethritis is also used. About half of NSU cases are caused by chlamydia (see pages 28-31).

NSU is a common problem and is usually easy to treat. It is spread through vaginal or anal sex. Many men who pick up these infections get no symptoms, so they are not classed as having NSU. But they can still pass the bacteria on to their partners, and for women their effects can be much more serious.

### Symptoms and effects

Symptoms begin 1-4 weeks after sex with an infected person. Peeing is painful and there is a clear or yellowish discharge from the penis, often most noticeable first thing in the morning. The opening of the urethra may be red and sore. Sometimes the man needs to pee more often. Oral or anal sex with an infected man or woman can cause soreness and discharge in the throat or anus.

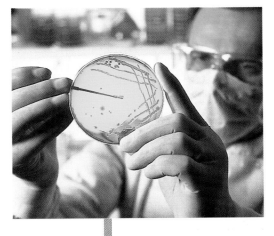

### Culture test
*A technician examines the bacteria growing on the jelly in a petri dish.*

Men do not usually suffer long-term effects from NSU. Occasionally they get a painful infection of an area inside the testicles called the epididymis, which in rare cases causes infertility if not treated.

### Testing and treatment

The doctor may diagnose NSU if a test for gonorrhoea is negative. NSU often clears up on its own. However, this does not always mean that the bacteria have disappeared. In most cases antibiotics will get rid of them completely. It's important to get treatment to avoid infecting female partners, who can suffer long-term effects including pain and infertility.

## Genital herpes

Genital herpes is caused by the herpes simplex virus, HSV. The virus exists in two types. HSV-1 usually infects the mouth and causes sores on the lips called cold sores or fever blisters; these are not usually sexually transmitted. HSV-2 usually infects the genital area, where it also causes sores. However, both types are capable of affecting either mouth or genitals.

HSV-2 is very widespread. In the USA, it lives in about 20 per cent of the population aged 13 or over. The 12-19 age group are now five times more likely to be infected than they were in the 1970s. Figures in Europe are thought to be similar. Once a person is infected, the virus stays in their body for life. It moves from the genitals or mouth and travels along the nerve cells to the base of the spinal cord, where it enters a resting state. In about 80 per cent of people it remains inactive permanently, or else reactivates from time to time but causes no recognizable symptoms. In the rest, reactivations cause outbreaks of painful sores.

HSV is spread by skin-to-skin contact at the affected area. This can happen through vaginal or anal sex – even if the penis touches the partner's genitals or anus but does not go inside. It can also be passed on through kissing or oral sex with someone who has cold sores on the mouth. It is spread during periods when the virus is active, but often people don't realize they are infectious because they don't have symptoms. Using a condom reduces the chance of infection but does not give complete protection, because

### Herpes virus
*A cross-section of a herpes virus. The inner ball is a protein coat containing the viral DNA, and is surrounded by a protective envelope.*

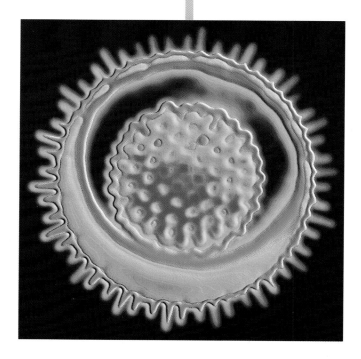

the infectious area may be outside the zone covered
by the condom.

Although it is not life-threatening, herpes
is an upsetting disease. Affected people
often feel anxious about sexual
relationships, fearing that they will infect
others or be rejected by present or future partners.
However, if couples are careful, an uninfected partner
can remain free of herpes even during a relationship
lasting many years.

*'It feels like I've got a dirty secret.
Nobody's going to want to have sex with
me now. Maybe I just won't tell
anyone I've got herpes.'*
*(Paul, 18)*

## Symptoms and effects

About 80 per cent of people who are infected with HSV-2
are unaware of their infection. Symptoms are either non-
existent or so mild that they are not recognized. When
symptoms do occur, they are usually most severe when
infection first happens, and begin 2-10 days after contact
with the virus. The first sign is often itching, tingling or
soreness in the genital area. Sores start as small, red
patches, which turn into painful blisters and
then open sores. In men they occur on the
penis, and in women on the vulva, inside the
vagina or on the cervix. In either sex the
anus and buttocks can also be affected. After
a few days a crust forms on the sores, and
after ten days they have usually healed.
During the first outbreak the person may
have headache, fever, muscle aches and
swelling of the glands in the groin.

After the first outbreak, symptoms return
periodically. The average is four or five times
a year, but for some people it is not so often.
The symptoms are usually less severe than
the first outbreak and last about a week.
Some people only get the itching and tingling
and don't develop sores. Over a few years,
outbreaks usually get less frequent.

### Herpes blisters
*Herpes blisters are
shallow, punched-out
ulcers, 2-3 mm across,
and extremely sore.*

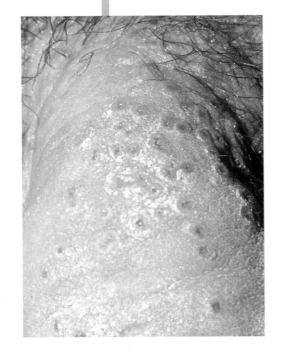

Pregnant women with active herpes can spread the virus to their babies during birth. This is most likely if the woman is infected for the first time during pregnancy. If not treated immediately, the baby may suffer brain damage or die. Infection of the baby can be prevented if it is born by caesarean section (when the baby is lifted out through a cut made in the mother's abdomen).

## Testing and treatment

Herpes is diagnosed after the doctor has examined the sores and taken details of other symptoms and sexual activity. To confirm the diagnosis, the infected area is wiped with a cotton wool swab, which is sent to a laboratory to see if HSV is present.

There is no cure for herpes. However, drugs are available that make the virus easier to live with. They do not remove HSV from the body, but they interfere with its reproduction. If taken at the first sign of symptoms, the drugs make the outbreak shorter and less severe. People whose outbreaks are very frequent can prevent at least 75 per cent of attacks by taking the drugs every day. But this is not a permanent solution, as they cannot be taken for life.

**Abstaining**
*Having to avoid sex during an outbreak of herpes can put a strain on relationships.*

People with herpes should avoid sexual contact during an outbreak, waiting until the sores are completely healed to reduce the risk of infecting their partner.

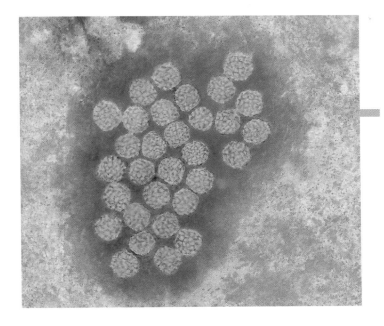

### Human papilloma viruses (HPV)

*Each human papilloma virus is icosahedral (twenty-sided). HPV is probably the most common sexually transmitted disease in the world.*

## Genital warts/human papilloma virus

Genital warts are caused by the human papilloma virus (HPV). There are over 90 types of HPV, many of which are spread non-sexually. Some cause warts on the hands and feet. About 20-30 of the types infect the genital area and are caught through sexual contact; sometimes they result in noticeable genital warts and sometimes they don't. As well as warts, HPV can sometimes cause cancer of the cervix. Once someone is infected, the virus may stay in their body for life.

HPV is probably the commonest sexually transmitted disease in the world. Scientists in the USA estimate that 80 per cent of sexually active people will be infected at some time in their life, but most will never show symptoms. In the UK, genital warts resulting from HPV are

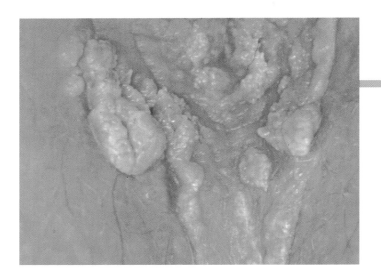

**Genital warts**
*The warts sometimes grow into raised areas with a rough surface.*

the most common problem diagnosed at STD clinics. As with many other STDs, the 16-24 age group has the highest rate of infection.

The virus is spread by skin-to-skin contact of the penis with the vagina or anus, and can be passed on even when there is no penetration. Infection through oral sex is rare. Warts on other parts of the body come from a different type of HPV and cannot spread to the genitals. Using a condom does not prevent HPV because the condom may not cover the whole of the infectious area; however, it does reduce the risk.

Visible genital warts are very contagious: sexual partners of affected people have a 60-70 per cent chance of getting HPV themselves. People without visible symptoms can still pass the virus on, but scientists are not sure how contagious it is in this group.

### Symptoms and effects

For most people, HPV is harmless and produces no symptoms. The virus moves to the deep layers of the skin, where it may remain inactive for months, years or even for life. In some people it becomes active and returns to the skin surface, where it often produces tiny spots of damage that are too small to see or feel.

In other cases it causes warts. These start as tiny swellings that often appear in clusters. The clusters can be small or can cover a larger area. Sometimes the warts remain small and disappear on their own after several months or years. In other cases they grow into rough, raised areas that look like the surface of a cauliflower. In men they can occur anywhere on the penis, and occasionally on the scrotum. In women they can appear on the vulva, inside the vagina, on the cervix or on the skin around the anus and on the perineum (the skin between the anus and the vagina). The anus can be affected in either sex.

*'After I had warts the doctor said I should have a smear test every year. Then if I do get any changes to my cervix, they can be treated before they get serious.'*
*(Alison, 16)*

## Testing and treatment

Doctors usually diagnose genital warts by their appearance. If a woman has warts the doctor will also check inside the vagina and at the cervix, using a

## HPV and cervical cancer

*A few types of HPV live on a woman's cervix and cause changes in the cells which can lead to cervical cancer. Often there are no warts so the woman does not know she is infected. Scientists now think that almost all cases of this cancer are caused by HPV. However, cancer only develops in a small minority of infected women. All sexually active women should have regular cervical smear tests (also called pap tests) to check for pre-cancerous changes, whether or not they have had genital warts. If caught early, nearly all cases of cervical cancer can be prevented or cured. Very rarely, HPV can cause cancer of the penis.*

magnifying glass called a colposcope. The warts are treated in different ways depending on their size and where they are. Treatment can be unpleasant, and after discussion with their doctor some people decide they would rather leave the warts as they are. Most will eventually clear up on their own, but this can take months or years.

Warts can be removed by freezing, burning or laser treatment, or cut out under local anaesthetic. There are also a range of drugs and chemicals which can be put on as creams or liquids. Never use treatments designed for hand or foot warts, as these could damage the delicate tissue of the genital area.

Even when the warts are removed, HPV remains in the body. Many people find the warts come back at least once, and perhaps several times. However, they usually come back less frequently as time passes. Someone whose warts have recently been treated might still be infectious, because the virus can still be active in the surrounding skin.

## Trichomoniasis

Trichomoniasis is caused by a tiny, single-celled parasite called *Trichomonas vaginalis*. It is almost always spread by vaginal sex, but it is also possible to catch it from wet towels or washcloths that have been used by an infected person. It is a common STD, affecting around 20 per cent of women at some time in their lives and producing 2-3 million cases in the USA alone each year. It is sometimes called 'trich' (pronounced 'trike'). It lives mainly in the vagina in women and in the urethra and bladder in men.

### Symptoms and effects

Trichomoniasis does not usually cause symptoms in men. When it does it produces a frothy or pus-like white discharge from the penis, pain when peeing and a need to pee more frequently. This is sometimes classed as non-

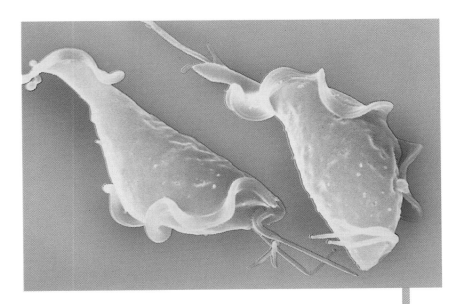

specific urethritis (NSU, see page 35). Very occasionally it causes a painful infection of an area inside the testicles called the epididymis. In rare cases, this causes infertility if not treated.

Symptoms are more common in women. They show up between 4 and 20 days after infection in the form of a frothy, yellowish-green vaginal discharge that may have an unpleasant or fishy smell. The vaginal area may be red, sore or itchy. Peeing or having sex may be painful, and the woman may need to pee more often.

## Testing and treatment

In women, the parasite can be detected by looking at a sample of vaginal liquid under a microscope. It is harder to detect in men, so a sample of penile discharge or urine may have to be sent away to a laboratory.

Trichomoniasis is treated with a drug called metronidazole, which kills the parasites. It is important to treat both sexual partners, otherwise they will re-infect each other.

# 5 Other STDs
## Causes, symptoms and treatment

The diseases covered in this chapter are less common than those in chapter 4, at least in the developed world. But they are still caught by thousands of people each year. Three of them – HIV (which causes AIDS), hepatitis B and syphilis – are the most dangerous of all the STDs.

**Myth**
*AIDS is a gay disease.*

**Fact**
*Sex between men and women accounts for 80-90 per cent of the world's HIV infections.*

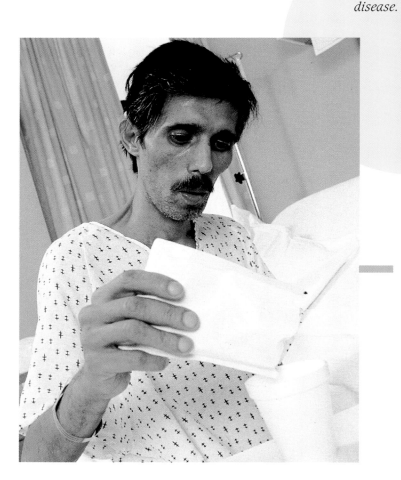

**Wasting**
*AIDS is causing the gradual wasting of this man's body.*

Patterns of disease are different around the world, and there are several other STDs that are a problem in the developing world but very uncommon elsewhere. There is not room to describe them in this book. Anyone who has been sexually active in other parts of the world, or whose partner has been, should consult their doctor if they are worried about symptoms of any kind.

## HIV and AIDS

AIDS stands for Acquired Immunodeficiency Syndrome and is caused by the Human Immunodeficiency Virus or HIV. Immunodeficiency means that the body's immune system is not working properly, so that the affected person cannot fight off infections in the normal way. Most people with AIDS eventually die from one of the infections they have caught.

AIDS is a new disease that was only given a name in 1982. It was first noticed in the late 1970s, when gay men in California and New York began to suffer in growing numbers from rare types of pneumonia, cancer and infections. In 1983 scientists identified the virus that was causing AIDS, and it was later named HIV. The virus is thought to have originated in Africa, where it is now much more common than in the developed world. It is also a serious problem in parts of Asia.

In the USA it is thought that between 650,000 and 900,000 people are infected with HIV. Up to a third of them do not realize that they have the virus. In the UK about 30,000 people are infected, and 2,500 new cases are diagnosed each year. Once HIV enters the body it stays there for life. The person becomes infectious straight away.

### An infected cell

*This false-colour electron micrograph shows a white blood cell, whose lumpy surface is a sign that it is infected with HIV. Virus particles (red) are budding from the cell membrane. HIV infects a key type of white cell, leading to the destruction of the immune system.*

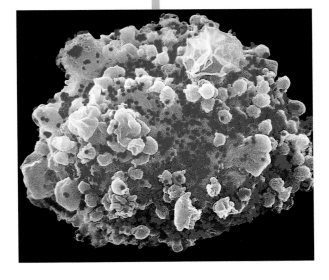

HIV is present in the blood, semen (sperm) and vaginal fluids. It is also in the fluid given out by the penis before ejaculation (pre-come), and in breast milk. It is passed on when any of these fluids gets inside another person's body. This can happen during vaginal, oral or anal sex, and most cases of HIV are sexually transmitted. Using a condom properly gives very good protection against HIV.

The virus can also be caught through sharing needles (when using drugs, body piercing or tattooing), blood transfusions (in countries where blood is not treated) or if infected blood gets into a cut in another person's skin. It cannot get through undamaged skin. Mothers can pass the virus to their babies before or during birth or while breastfeeding.

### Who gets HIV?

Around the world, most HIV infections are passed on by sex between men and women (heterosexual sex). However, patterns of infection vary between countries. In the developed world, sex between men has so far been responsible for the largest number of cases. But the rate of infection from heterosexual sex is rising. In the UK in

### Infected from birth

*These young children in a South African orphanage have picked up HIV from their mothers, who have since died of AIDS. A devastating epidemic of HIV has swept through many parts of Africa.*

# Risk groups for HIV

*Anyone who is sexually active can get HIV (unless neither partner has ever had sex with anyone else). But in the developed world, the risk of infection is higher for these groups:*

- *Men who have sex with men (both homosexuals and bisexuals)*
- *People who inject drugs*
- *People who have been sexually active in countries where HIV is common, especially South, East and Central Africa*
- *Sexual partners of any of the above groups*

*Infection rates in other groups are rising. Everyone should protect themselves against HIV and other STDs – see pages 14-19 for advice on how.*

1999, more people caught HIV heterosexually than homosexually. Most of the heterosexual infections were probably picked up during travel to countries where the virus is more common.

## AIDS/HIV and young people

- So far, HIV is rare in heterosexual British teenagers. In 1998, fewer than 1 in 1,000 were infected when STD clinics did tests on clients in this age group.
- In the USA, 1998 saw nearly 2,000 new cases of AIDS in people aged 13-24. Half had been infected through gay male sex and 10 per cent through injecting drugs. Many of the rest caught it heterosexually, although full information was not available.
- Half of all HIV infections reported in 13-24 year-olds in the USA in 1998 were in women. In the 13-19 age group, women accounted for 62 per cent of the infections reported.

## Symptoms and effects

Some people get flu-like symptoms in the first two months after infection. These usually involve fever, headache and swollen glands in the neck and groin, and clear up in 1-4 weeks. Others experience nothing at all. The person then stays fit and well for an average of 10 years. During this time the virus is silently multiplying and destroying the white blood cells known as T4, which play a key role in the immune system. As this system becomes weaker, many people go through months or years of lesser symptoms before they develop full-blown AIDS. These include:

- swollen glands
- fevers and night sweats
- rashes
- frequent yeast (thrush) or herpes infections
- tiredness
- weight loss

AIDS is the final stage of HIV. The person begins to suffer from a range of infections, many from everyday bacteria, viruses and fungi that are harmless to healthy people. Symptoms caused by these infections include:

- coughs
- pneumonia (serious lung infection)
- severe diarrhoea, vomiting or stomach cramps
- severe headaches
- problems with the eyesight and eventually blindness
- confusion, forgetfulness and loss of coordination
- certain cancers, especially Kaposi's sarcoma which affects the blood vessels and appears as skin blotches

Sometimes people are able to lead almost normal lives between illnesses, but they risk a fatal infection at any time. Others steadily lose weight and get very tired and weak. Many become unable to work or look after themselves. Eventually they die from one of their infections.

## Testing and treatment

When someone is infected with HIV they produce antibodies in an unsuccessful attempt to get rid of the virus. Antibodies are made by the immune system to recognize and help destroy particular viruses or bacteria. Infection is diagnosed using a blood test that looks for antibodies to HIV. People who have them are described as HIV-positive. Antibodies take about three months to develop, so it is possible for a recently infected person to come out negative in the test.

### Holiday camp

*People with HIV remain healthy for many years before developing AIDS. Thanks to new drugs, many who were previously sick can lead active lives again, though there is still no cure. These girls are at a US holiday camp for young people who have HIV or AIDS.*

### Ellen

*Ellen discovered she was HIV positive when she was 16. She went for a test when she found out that her boyfriend's previous girlfriend was a drug user and had developed AIDS. 'I didn't expect the test to be positive,' she remembers. 'When it was, it felt like being given a death sentence. For months I was just numb, I couldn't take it in.'*

*Now, three years on, she is at college and is enjoying life. She has recently started taking a combination of drugs to keep the HIV virus under control. 'I'm on 24 pills a day, and they've all got to be taken at the right times. It's hard to get used to, and sometimes they make me feel really sick. But I know they're my best hope. I try not to think about the future too much; I just concentrate on today and try to get as much out of life as I can.'*

New drugs mean that it is now possible to slow down HIV's reproduction and thus keep the immune system functioning for longer. People with HIV are therefore staying healthy for much longer than before: in the UK, the death rate from AIDS fell by two-thirds between 1995 and 1999. To keep the virus under control it is necessary to take a combination of several drugs, several times a day, for life. Sticking to this schedule is not easy, and these powerful medicines can have unpleasant side effects. A major problem is HIV's ability to become resistant to drugs, so that they are no longer effective. The person then has to try another drug combination, and some people have run out of treatments that work for them. Drugs are also available to treat some of the infections that affect people with AIDS. The new treatments have made little difference in the developing world because most people cannot afford them.

## Hepatitis B

Hepatitis means inflammation of the liver. It is often caused by viruses, and one of these – hepatitis B – can be passed on through sex. Scientists now believe that the hepatitis C virus, which is less common, can probably spread sexually as well. Both can cause serious illness.

The hepatitis B virus (HBV) lives in the blood, sperm and vaginal fluid of infected people. It is spread when these enter the body of another person. As well as during sex, this can happen when drug users share needles, or through other contact with infected blood. A tiny amount of blood, too small to see, is enough to pass the virus on. Pregnant women can pass hepatitis B to their babies.

### Needles
*Drug users are at risk from hepatitis B and HIV if they share needles with an infected person.*

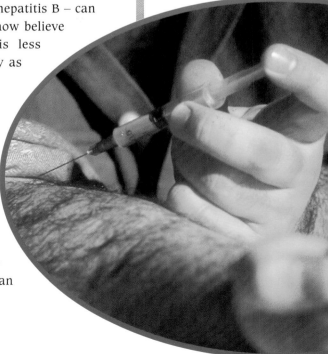

In the USA between 140,000 and 320,000 people become infected with HBV each year. About half get symptoms. The rest do not realize they are infected, but can still pass HBV to other people.

People at most risk from getting HBV sexually are those who have more than one sexual partner in six months and men who have sex with men. Using condoms properly reduces the risk of catching HBV. There is also a safe and effective vaccine, which in the USA has been given to babies since 1991 and to 10-11 year-olds since 1995. It takes three injections to be fully effective. If you are worried you should check whether you've had the vaccine, or discuss vaccination with your doctor.

### Symptoms and effects

Some people get no symptoms from HBV. Those who do usually get flu-like symptoms, which can be mild and short-lived or can make them feel very ill, with lost appetite, nausea and vomiting and often a fever. There may be pain in the stomach or joints. After a few days jaundice may develop: this is due to problems with liver function and can make the skin and eyes look yellow and the urine turn dark. It can take 4-8 weeks to recover fully. In a few cases the liver is seriously affected or fails completely, leading to dangerous illness or death. People who have had hepatitis B can feel very tired for weeks or months afterwards.

## Hepatitis B carriers

Some people never get rid of the virus, even when their symptoms get better. These people – known as carriers – are infectious to others for the rest of their lives. There are about 1 million carriers in the USA – about 1 in 250 people. In the UK the figure is about 1 in 1,000, rising to about 1 in 50 in areas where a lot of people were born in high-risk countries.

In 5-10 per cent of cases, hepatitis B becomes chronic. This means the liver stays inflamed for months or years. Some people feel no effects, while others feel constantly tired and ill. Sometimes the liver slowly becomes more and more damaged until it can no longer work and the person dies. There is also an increased risk of liver cancer.

### Testing and treatment

Hepatitis B is diagnosed using a blood test. There is no cure, but most cases get better on their own. People with chronic hepatitis which is getting worse can sometimes be helped with drugs, but these are expensive and often have side effects.

## Syphilis

Syphilis was first described in Europe at the end of the fifteenth century, and has been known in North America since the time of Columbus. It spread quickly and became a much-feared epidemic. However, since the Second World War the number of cases in the industrialized world has fallen sharply, and syphilis is now rare.
In the UK there were just 128 new cases in 1998, about half of which were picked up abroad. The problem is greater in parts of the USA, especially among poorer African-American communities in the south-east of the country, who find it difficult to get access to affordable healthcare. Men who have sex with men also have a greater risk of syphilis. There were almost 38,000 reported cases in the USA in 1998.

Syphilis is caused by bacteria called *Treponema pallidum*. It spreads through direct contact between a syphilis sore and the moist lining of the genitals, mouth or anus of a sexual partner. Using a condom properly gives good protection against syphilis infection. The bacteria cannot pass through the skin on the rest of the body, unless it is broken. Pregnant women with syphilis can pass the infection to their unborn babies.

### An Inca model
*The Inca civilization in South America was discovered and conquered by Spain in the sixteenth century. This Inca model represents someone infected with syphilis.*

## *Symptoms and effects*

Syphilis is a complicated disease that is divided into four stages. It is infectious during the first two.

- Stage 1 (primary syphilis): a single, small sore called a chancre (pronounced shanker) appears on the infected area between 10 and 90 days after infection. Because the sore is usually painless and can be inside the body, many people do not notice it. The chancre heals on its own in 1-5 weeks, but if the infection is not treated it progresses to stage 2.

- Stage 2 (secondary syphilis): 3-6 weeks after the chancre appears, the person gets a rash on the skin. This is often made up of rough, brownish spots which appear on the palms of the hands, the soles of the feet and sometimes other parts of the body. However, the rash can also look like a heat rash. If the infection is in the mouth it creates slimy, white patches. The rash disappears after 2-6 weeks. Some people get flu-like symptoms at this stage. Secondary syphilis can last as long as two years, during which time the symptoms come and go.

- If syphilis is not treated it progresses to the latent (hidden) stage. The bacteria remain in the body but are no longer infectious. About two-thirds of people have no further symptoms.

- In about a third of people, the bacteria slowly damage the internal organs and nervous system over a period of many years. As the damage worsens it causes a range of serious symptoms that can include paralysis, blindness, insanity, heart disease, bone and joint damage, and chronic vomiting and abdominal pain. This is called tertiary or late syphilis, and can be fatal.

**Secondary syphilis**
*A rash on the palms of the hands is very often a symptom of stage 2 of syphilis.*

Babies born to mothers with untreated syphilis have a 40-70 per cent chance of being infected. This is called congenital syphilis. Many are stillborn or die soon after

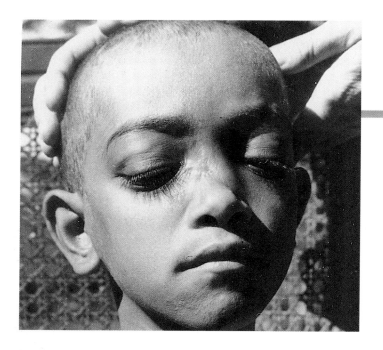

## Congenital syphilis

*This child in India has congenital syphilis. The infection was passed on by his mother at birth.*

birth. Unless they are treated quickly, they may develop serious or fatal illness and may be left mentally retarded.

## Testing and treatment

Syphilis has been called 'the great imitator', because its early symptoms can easily be confused with other diseases. It's therefore important for sexually active people to see a doctor about any suspicious sores or rashes. Syphilis can be diagnosed by looking at a sample from the chancre under a microscope to check for the Treponema bacteria. The doctor usually uses a blood test as well; if the first test is positive, a second test is given to confirm the result.

Syphilis can be cured with penicillin or certain other antibiotics at all stages of the infection. This kills the bacteria, leaving the person syphilis-free and not infectious. However, antibiotics cannot repair any damage that has been done to the internal organs in someone with the late-stage disease. It is important that all sexual partners are notified so that they can be treated as well.

The infections described on pages 55-59 are all transmitted through sexual contact, but can also be transmitted in other ways.

## Bacterial vaginosis

Bacterial vaginosis (BV) is a common problem which happens when the normal balance of bacteria in the vagina is disturbed. Normally the vagina is dominated by beneficial bacteria which give off a natural disinfectant, but sometimes these are overpowered by unwanted and potentially harmful species. Sex seems to play a role in BV because it is most common in sexually active women, especially if they have recently changed partners. However, researchers are still trying to understand exactly what causes BV to develop. It can affect women who have never had sex. BV should not be confused with thrush (candidiasis), which is caused by yeast microbes and is not sexually transmitted.

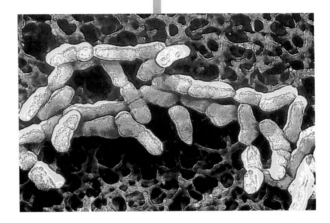

**Gardnerella**

*These rod-shaped gardnerella bacteria are one of the types associated with BV.*

### Symptoms and effects

BV causes an abnormal vaginal discharge. It is thin and milky-white or grey in colour, and is usually heavier than the normal vaginal secretions. It has an unpleasant smell which is described as fishy or musty. The smell is often especially noticeable after sex, when the vaginal fluids are mixed with semen. Some women feel an itching or burning sensation in the vagina. Nearly half of women with BV do not realize that anything is wrong; the condition is only noticed when they have a vaginal examination for some other reason, perhaps at an STD clinic.

It is important to treat BV because it is linked to an increased risk of pelvic inflammatory disease (see page 30), which can cause pain and infertility.

### Testing and treatment

BV makes the vaginal secretions more acidic. This can easily be detected in the surgery or clinic using pH paper. Some doctors do this test whenever they give a vaginal examination. The doctor may also look at a sample of vaginal fluid under the microscope, or may add an alkaline substance to the fluid to show up any fishy smell.

BV is treated with antibiotics, either as tablets or as pessaries placed in the vagina. The doctor will use specific antibiotic types which target the harmful bacteria while leaving the protective ones alone.

## Molluscum contagiosum

Molluscum contagiosum is a common skin infection caused by the molluscum contagiosum virus. It is spread by all types of skin-to-skin contact and through sharing items such as towels or clothing with an infected person. It may also be passed on through shared baths and possibly swimming pools. Sexual contact is the most common way of catching molluscum contagiosum for adults.

### Symptoms and effects

Molluscum contagiosum appears as small, round bumps on the skin. These can be pearly-white, yellow or flesh-coloured, and can range from a few millimetres to 3-4 centimetres across. The usual size is less than 1 centimetre. The bumps often have a soft, sunken centre. They are not usually painful, though they are sometimes itchy or tender. If the infection has been caught sexually, the areas affected are the groin, thighs, buttocks or genitals – though not usually the penis or the inside of the vagina. The bumps appear in anything from a few weeks to six months after contact with the infected person or object.

There are no long-term effects from molluscum contagiosum. The bumps usually disappear by themselves, but this can take up to four years. An infected person can spread the virus around their body by touching the bumps and then touching other areas.

### Testing and treatment

Molluscum contagiosum can usually be diagnosed by the appearance of the bumps, but if in doubt the doctor will send a small piece of skin for examination under a microscope. Although it is not dangerous, doctors usually recommend treating the infection to stop it spreading around the body or being passed to others. Anyway, many people want the bumps removed because they find them embarrassing.

Treatment involves removing the individual bumps. This can be done by freezing them, burning them off with a special chemical or treating them with electricity.

## Pubic lice ('crabs')

Pubic lice are parasitic insects that live in the pubic hair (the hair surrounding the genitals). They may also settle in armpit and chest hair and even the eyelashes, but not usually on the head. They look like tiny crabs – hence their popular nickname. They are related to head lice but belong to a different species. Head lice don't infect the genital area. Pubic lice are common all over the world, and infection rates are on the increase.

Pubic lice are the most contagious of all STDs. Someone who has sex with an infected person just once has a 95 per cent chance of catching them. They can spread any time that pubic hair touches, not just during full sex. They can also survive for 1-2 days away from the body, so you could pick them up from bedding or towels used by an infected person. They cannot live on toilet seats.

### Pubic lice

*Pubic lice feed on blood and lay their eggs in the pubic hair. Each female lays about 50 eggs, which take 7-10 days to hatch. This electron micrograph shows an egg hatching.*

## Symptoms and effects

You may not notice anything for up to four weeks after catching lice, depending on how many of the parasites you picked up. The main symptom is itching in the genital area. This can be very intense. You will know it is due to lice because you can see them in the hair. Sometimes you can also see the bite marks, which are small and bluish in colour. There are no long-term effects from pubic lice.

## Testing and treatment

There is no test for lice as the doctor can see them with the naked eye. If you have lice there is a chance you may have caught another STD as well, so it's a good idea to ask your doctor or clinic about other tests.

*'Crabs sounds like a joke, but it wasn't funny. The itching drove me crazy and the thought of having lice on my body was disgusting. I felt so dirty.'*
*(Marcia, 15)*

Pubic lice can be treated with several different shampoos and creams; some need a prescription from a doctor but some can be bought directly from a pharmacist. Follow the instructions on the packet. All clothing, bedding and towels used in the two days before treatment should be washed. The itching can last for a few days after the lice have been killed. If the lice have not gone after a week, see your doctor.

## Scabies

Scabies is a skin infection caused by a microscopic animal called *Sarcoptes scabei*, also known as the itch mite. It is common all over the world, and spreads by prolonged skin-to-skin contact. This can happen during sex or while sleeping in the same bed as your partner. It also spreads non-sexually among people living in the same house and in places like hospitals and childcare nurseries. Scabies can be caught from shared clothes, towels or bedding, where the mites can live for up to three days.

The female scabies mite burrows down into the skin to lay its eggs, which hatch a few days later into larvae. These work their way to the surface and keep the infection going.

## Symptoms and effects

The main symptom is intense itching, which is usually worse at night. The itching is caused by an allergic reaction to the mite. You can often see the burrows that the mites have made, which appear as wavy lines about a centimetre long. Some people also get itchy, reddish pimples and bumps. The main areas affected are the webs between the fingers, the wrists, elbows, armpits, breasts (women), genitals and buttocks. The itching can be so bad that the person develops skin sores from scratching, and these sometimes get infected with bacteria.

For the first infection with scabies, symptoms take 4-6 weeks to appear. If someone is infected again the itching starts sooner, because the body 'remembers' the previous allergic reaction to the mites. Scabies does not have any long-term effects.

## Testing and treatment

The doctor can usually tell if a person has scabies just by hearing about the itching and looking for the burrows. Sometimes he or she will look at a scraping of the skin under a microscope to check for mites, though these cannot always be found. Most people with scabies have fewer than ten mites on their whole body.

There are several lotions and creams available to treat scabies. Some have to be left on for eight hours before washing off. After treatment you should put on clean clothes and wash all towels, clothes and bedding used in the last two days. You may need to use the lotion again 7-10 days later. Itching can last for 2-3 weeks after treatment has killed the mites. Sexual partners and people who live in the same house as an infected person should also be treated.

**An itch mite**
*This false-colour electron micrograph shows a scabies (itch) mite on the surface of the skin. Itch mites' saliva or faeces cause an allergic reaction, which makes the skin itch intensely.*

# Glossary

| | |
|---|---|
| anal sex | when the penis enters the anus, either of a woman or of another man. |
| antibiotics | drugs that kill bacteria. |
| antibodies | proteins made by the immune system to fight specific infections. |
| anus | the opening at the end of the digestive tract (the bum hole or butt hole). |
| bisexual | attracted to or having sex with people of both sexes. |
| cervical cancer | cancer of the cervix (the opening or neck of the uterus). |
| cervix | the opening of the uterus (womb), found at the top of the vagina. |
| chronic | lasting a long time (months or years) – to describe a disease or symptom. |
| condom | rubber or plastic sheath that fits over the penis to prevent pregnancy and STDs. Female condoms are rubber or plastic sheets worn inside the vagina. (Unlike caps or diaphragms, they cover the whole vagina.) |
| contagious | (easily) spread by skin-to-skin contact. |
| contraceptive | drug or device used to prevent pregnancy. |
| diagnosis | identification of a disease using symptoms or tests. |

| | |
|---|---|
| discharge | release of pus or fluid from a part of the body. |
| DNA | deoxyribonucleic acid, the genetic material of nearly all living things. |
| ejaculation | the release of semen from the penis. |
| electron micrograph | an image obtained using an electron microscope, a powerful instrument that gives extremely high magnification. In 'false-colour' images, the colours are put in by computer to show up particular features. |
| faithful | a faithful relationship is one where the partners do not have sex with anyone else. |
| Fallopian tubes | the tubes leading from the ovaries to the uterus. |
| gay | homosexual, i.e. attracted to people of the same sex. |
| genitals | the external sex organs. |
| heterosexual | attracted to or having sex with someone of the opposite sex. |
| homosexual | attracted to or having sex with someone of the same sex. |
| immune system | the body's natural defences against infection, made up of special blood cells and messenger chemicals. |
| infectious | spread from one person to another; (of a person) capable of infecting other people. |

| | |
|---|---|
| infertile | unable to have children. |
| inflammation | swelling, often with pain and redness as well. |
| IVF | in vitro fertilization – a treatment for infertility where the egg is fertilized outside the body, then placed in the uterus. |
| oral sex | using the mouth to stimulate the partner's genitals. |
| ovaries | the female organs that produce eggs. |
| parasites | animals that live on and get their food from humans or other animals, e.g. lice. |
| penetration | when the penis enters the vagina or anus. |
| pessary | a dissolving tablet inserted into the vagina to deliver medication. |
| prostitute | someone who has sex for money. |

| | |
|---|---|
| rectum | the end of the digestive tract, just inside the anus. |
| scrotum | the sack that contains the testicles (balls). |
| semen | the fluid containing sperm. |
| sexually active | taking part in physical sexual relationships. |
| smear test | test used to detect changes in the cells of the cervix that could lead to cancer. |
| symptoms | the physical effects produced by a disease, e.g. rash, pain, fever. |
| unprotected sex | sex without a condom. |
| uterus | womb. |
| vaginal sex | when the penis enters the vagina. |
| vulva | the area around the vaginal opening. |

ovaries 22, 30, 31, 34

parasites 5, 12, 26
  pubic lice 5, 57, 58
  *Sarcoptes scabei* (scabies)
  12, 58, 59
  *Trichomonas vaginalis* 42,
  43
peeing 21, 22, 24, 29, 33, 35,
  42, 43
pelvic inflammatory disease
  (PID) 26, 30, 31, 32, 34, 55
penis 5, 12, 13, 17, 21, 28,
  29, 32, 33, 34, 35, 36, 37,
  40, 41, 42, 46, 56
perineum 41
pregnancy 11, 15, 16, 18, 30,
  31, 38, 50, 52
prostate gland 21
prostitution 8, 9, 32
pubic lice 5, 12, 13, 57-58

rectum 21, 22, 33
relationships 11, 14, 15, 16,
  17, 23, 37, 38

scabies 12, 13, 58-59
screening 11
scrotum 21, 31, 41
semen 5, 12, 46, 55
smear test 19, 34, 41
sperm 12, 13, 17, 46, 50
sperm duct 21
sexual behaviour
  abstinence 14-15, 38
  risky 9, 16
  safer sex 9, 15, 16, 18-19,
  25

STD clinics 10, 11, 19, 24,
  25, 27, 34, 40
STDs
  emotional effects 23, 27, 37
  risk groups 6, 8, 9, 10, 11,
  12, 16, 47, 50, 51, 52
  testing and treatment 11,
  19, 24, 25, 26, 27, 31, 32,
  34, 35, 36, 42, 43, 49, 50,
  52, 54, 56, 57, 58, 59
  young people 6, 10, 11, 19,
  29, 32, 36, 40, 47
STIs 4
swabs 24, 25, 32, 38
swimming pools 13, 56
symptoms of STDs 6, 8, 19,
  20, 21, 22, 23, 24, 26, 27,
  45
  AIDS/HIV 47-48
  bacterial vaginosis 55
  chlamydia 29-31
  genital herpes 36, 37-38
  genital warts (HPV) 39, 40,
  41
  gonorrhoea 33-34
  hepatitis B 51
  molluscum contagiosum 56
  NSU 35
  pubic lice 58
  scabies 59
  syphilis 53, 54
  trichomoniasis 42-43
syphilis 4, 5, 6, 11, 13, 32,
  44, 52-54
  congenital 53, 54

throat 21, 22, 26, 29, 35
thrush 55

toilet seats 13, 57
towels 13, 42, 56, 57, 58, 59
trichomoniasis 42-43

urethra 21, 22, 35, 42
urine test 24, 32, 34, 43
uterus 22, 30, 31, 34

vaccination, HBV 51
vagina 5, 12, 13, 19, 22, 29,
  33, 34, 37, 40, 41, 42, 43,
  55, 56
vaginal fluids 5, 12, 43, 46,
  50, 55, 56
vaginal sex 12, 18, 28, 32,
  35, 36, 42, 46
viruses 4, 5, 12, 20, 26-27,
  48, 49, 50
  hepatitis 27, 50, 51
  herpes 12, 26, 36, 37, 38
  HIV 4, 12, 26, 45, 46, 47,
  48, 49, 50
  human papilloma 11, 12,
  27, 39, 40, 42
  molluscum contagiosum 56,
  57
vulva 22, 37, 41